Bird Babies

Catherine Veitch

Raintree is an imprint of Capstone Global Library Limited, a company incorporated in England and Wales having its registered office at 7 Pilgrim Street, London, EC4V 6LB – Registered company number: 6695582

www.raintreepublishers.co.uk
myorders@raintreepublishers.co.uk

Text © Capstone Global Library Limited 2013
First published in hardback in 2013
Paperback edition first published in 2014
The moral rights of the proprietor have been asserted.

Edited by Daniel Nunn, Rebecca Rissman, and Catherine Veitch
Designed by Cynthia Della-Rovere
Picture research by Ruth Blair
Production by Victoria Fitzgerald
Originated by Capstone Global Library
Printed and bound in China

ISBN 978 1 406 25923 0 (hardback)
17 16 15 14 13
10 9 8 7 6 5 4 3 2 1

ISBN 978 1 406 25930 8 (paperback)
18 17 16 15 14
10 9 8 7 6 5 4 3 2 1

British Library Cataloguing in Publication Data
Veitch, Catherine.
Bird babies. -- (Animal babies)
598.1'39-dc23
A full catalogue record for this book is available from the British Library.

Acknowledgements
We would like to thank the following for permission to reproduce photographs:Corbis pp. title page (© Frank Krahmer), 17 (© Oanh/Image Source); Naturepl pp. 7 (© Yuri Shibnev), 9 (© Grzegorz Lesniewski), 13 (© Paul Johnson), 14 (© Mike Read), 15 (© Stephen Dalton), 19 (© Simon Wagen / J Downer Product), 21 (© Bernard Castelein), 23 (© Grzegorz Lesniewski, © Yuri Shibnev); Shutterstock pp. 4 (© Stephanie Dalen), 5 (© Jaroslaw Saternus), 6 (© Maksimilian), 8 (© Vishnevskiy Vasily), 10 (©Bambuh), 11 (© J.A.Astor), 12 (© Frank Pali), 16 (© Steve Byland), 18 (© Josh Anon), 20 (© Janneke Spronk), 22 (© Cheryl E. Davis, © Vishnevskiy Vasily, © Craig Barhorst, © thomas bonnefoy1), 23 (© rawcaptured).

Front cover photograph of an emperor penguin with chicks reproduced with kind permission of Corbis (© Frank Krahmer).

We would like to thank Michael Bright for his invaluable help in the preparation of this book.

Every effort has been made to contact copyright holders of material reproduced in this book. Any omissions will be rectified in subsequent printings if notice is given to the publisher.

Contents

What is a bird?

beak

feathers

A bird has a beak.

A bird has feathers.

wings

A bird has wings.
Most birds can fly.

How are baby birds born?

egg

Female birds lay eggs.

Some birds lay one egg at a time.

Some birds lay more than one egg
at a time.

Eggs can be different colours.

Eggs can be different sizes.

A baby bird hatches from each egg.

Some baby birds are born
with feathers.

Some baby birds are born with
no feathers.

Where do baby birds live?

Most baby birds live in nests.
Nests help keep them safe.

Some baby birds live in nests on the ground.

Some baby birds live in nests
on cliffs.

Some baby birds live in nests
in buildings.

What do baby birds eat?

Some baby birds are fed by their parents.

Many baby birds eat worms. Many baby birds eat seeds and berries.

Caring for eggs and baby birds

A bird protects its eggs and baby birds from predators.

oil

This bird spits a smelly oil at predators to scare them away.

Growing up

Baby birds learn to fly.

Sometimes they fall out of the nest.

Baby birds learn to find food.

Life cycle of a bird

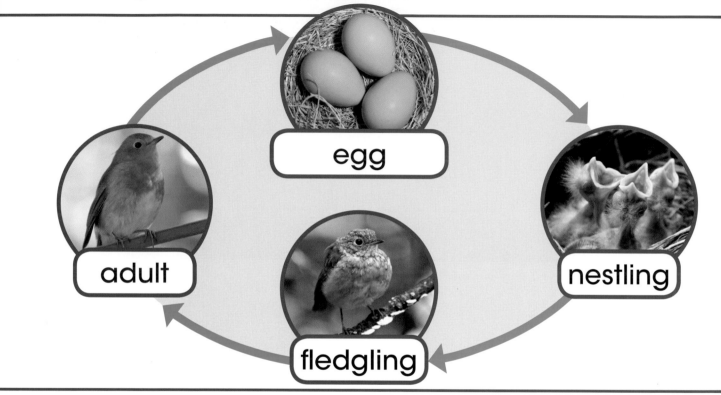

egg

adult

nestling

fledgling

A life cycle shows the different stages of an animal's life. This is the life cycle of a bird.

Picture glossary

 **female** animal that can give birth. Female birds lay eggs.

 **hatch** break out of an egg

 **predator** animal that eats other animals

Index

Notes for parents and teachers
Before reading

Show children a collection of photos and videos of birds. National Geographic and BBC Nature are useful websites. Explain what a bird is and discuss the characteristics of birds.

After reading

- Mount photos of adult and baby birds on card, and play games of snap and pairs where the children have to match a baby bird with its parent. Model the correct pairs first.

- Ask children to label the parts of a bird: for example, beak, feathers, wings, legs.

- Look at page 22 and discuss the life cycle stages of a bird. Mount photos of the egg, nestling, fledgling and adult stages and ask children to put the photos in order. Encourage children to draw a life cycle of a human to compare. Compare how different birds care for their babies. Discuss the care human babies need.

- To extend children's knowledge, the birds are as follows: peacock: p4; barn owl: p5; puffin: p6; finch eggs: p7; gull hatching: p9; emu: p10; blue tits: p11; hummingbird: p12; oystercatcher: p13; kittiwake: p14; swallows: p15; eastern bluebirds: p16; robin: p17; cormorants: p18; fulmar: p19; wagtail: p20; avocet: p21.